Developing and Scaling Social Media Business Ideas

Table of Contents

1. Introduction 2

2. Understanding the Power of Social Media 3

    2.1. Social Media: A Brief Run-down 3

    2.2. The All-encompassing Impact of Social Media 4

    2.3. Social Media as a Powerhouse for Businesses 4

    2.4. Unveiling the Potential of Social Media for Profit 5

    2.5. The Future is Social 5

3. The Premise of a Profitable Digital Venture 7

    3.1. Grasping the Essence of Social Media 7

    3.2. The Building Blocks of A Profitable Social Media Venture 8

    3.3. Unpacking The Social Media Revenue Model 8

4. Identifying Growth Opportunities in Social Media 10

    4.1. The Basis: Social Media Demographics 10

    4.2. Emergence of New Platforms and Features 10

    4.3. Recognition of Trends and Viral Content 11

    4.4. Socio-Political Climate's Interplay 11

    4.5. E-Commerce Capabilities and Monetization Paths 11

    4.6. Influencer Marketing: The Gigantic Wave 12

    4.7. Data Analytics: The Guiding Light 12

5. Innovative Social Media Business Ideas 13

    5.1. Leveraging Influencer Marketing 13

    5.2. Delving Into Social Media Consultancy 13

    5.3. Podcasting: The Rising Star 14

    5.4. Capitalizing on Gamification 14

    5.5. Harnessing User-Generated Content 15

    5.6. Penetrating E-commerce Via Social Media 15

    5.7. Social Media Management Tools 15

    5.8. Video-Based Learning Platforms 16

6. Strategizing for Social Media Success 17

   6.1. Identifying Your Goals and Linking them to Metrics 17

   6.2. Understanding Your Target Audience 18

   6.3. Competitor Analysis 18

   6.4. Content Creation and Curation 18

   6.5. Building a Social Media Calendar 19

   6.6. Adjusting Your Strategy through Analytics 19

7. Developing a Robust Business Model 20

   7.1. Constructing an Effective Social Media Business Model 20

   7.2. Identifying Your Target Audience 20

   7.3. Competition Analysis 21

   7.4. Building Your Unique Value Proposition (UVP) 21

   7.5. Deciding on Revenue Streams 22

   7.6. Developing a Scalable Model 22

8. Omnipresent Approach: Multichannel Social Media Marketing . . 24

   8.1. Grasping the Concept of Multichannel Social Media
Marketing 24

   8.2. The Importance of Multichannel Social Media Marketing . . . 25

   8.3. Constructing a Multichannel Social Media Marketing
Strategy 25

   8.4. Embracing Technological Tools for Effective Multichannel
Social Media Marketing 26

   8.5. Challenges and Solutions in Multichannel Social Media
Marketing 27

9. Scaling Techniques for Your Social Media Business 28

   9.1. Focusing on Your Target Audience 28

   9.2. Creating High-Quality, Engaging Content 28

   9.3. Establishing a Strong Social Media Branding 29

   9.4. Engaging with Your Audience 29

   9.5. Utilizing the Power of Influencer Marketing 29

9.6. Leverage Algorithm Changes 30

10. Sustaining Growth Amidst Social Media Algorithm Changes . . . 31

10.1. Understanding the Impact of Algorithm Changes 31

10.2. Adapting to the Changing Algorithms 31

10.2.1. Developing Adaptive Content 32

10.2.2. Customer-Centric Approach 32

10.2.3. Diversifying Social Media Portfolio 32

10.3. Navigating through Algorithm Updates 32

10.3.1. Staying Informed 32

10.3.2. Experimentation and A/B Testing 33

10.3.3. Measuring Performance 33

10.4. Ensuring Sustainable Growth Amidst Change 33

10.4.1. Building a Strong Community 33

10.4.2. Leveraging User-Generated Content 34

10.4.3. Paid Advertising 34

11. The Future of Social Media Business 35

11.1. A Look Into the Crystal Ball: Upcoming Trends in Social
Media 35

11.2. Adapting to the Social Media Business Landscape: The
New Gameplan 36

11.3. Future-proofing Your Social Media Business Against
Algorithm Changes 37

Your culture is your brand. On social media, people want to see consistency and authenticity; that's what will make the experience feel real for them and engage them in your mission and vision.

Chapter 1. Introduction

Unleash the Power of Social Media! Welcome to our special report: "Developing and Scaling Social Media Business Ideas". Prepare to take a captivating ride through the dynamic world of social media; unravel its potential for profit, and understand its ability to revolutionize businesses across scales. Whether you are an established business trying to amplify your digital presence, or an ambitious entrepreneur looking for groundbreaking ideas and strategies to scale on these platforms, this report is tailored for you. With a novel blend of case studies, expert analysis, step-by-step guides, and actionable insights, you won't want to miss out on this opportunity to take your venture to new heights. Excited? So are we! Discover the path to social media success and immerse yourself in this transformative business journey. Order your copy of the special report today and meet your future at the doorstep of social media prowess!

Chapter 2. Understanding the Power of Social Media

Consider the diverse world we live in: staggering seven billion people, more than five thousand languages spoken, countless cultures and behaviors exhibited. Now consider a platform that connects this diverse populace, transcending geographical, cultural, and linguistic boundaries. That platform, dear reader, is Social Media.

The speed and pervasiveness with which social media has permeated our lives are unprecedented. What started as virtual forums for connecting with people and sharing interests has evolved into a powerful tool impacting our lives at all levels - be it social, political, or economic.

2.1. Social Media: A Brief Run-down

Before delving deeper, let's briefly trace the journey of social media. In essence, social media platforms are digital spaces that enable users to create and share content or to participate in social networking. Platforms like Facebook, Twitter, Instagram, LinkedIn, and YouTube have radically transformed how we live our lives and do business.

While the beginnings of social media date back to the bulletin board systems of the 1970s, the first recognizable social media site, Six Degrees, appeared in 1997. Then came services like Blogger, LinkedIn, and Facebook that set strong foundations. We then saw the proliferation of photo sharing platforms such as Flickr and Instagram, followed by platforms like Twitter that thrived on real-time interaction. Today, with numerous new players augmenting users' experiences (like TikTok, Clubhouse, etc.), the social media landscape is more vibrant than ever.

2.2. The All-encompassing Impact of Social Media

Social media has significantly reshaped our relationships and communication styles. Its potential for collaboration and real-time interaction has democratized content creation, consumption, and virality, breaking down the conventional gate-keeping paradigms.

Social media's influence extends well beyond personal life. It has altered the business landscape dramatically, introducing a paradigm shift in how businesses interact with their customers. Brands have harnessed the power of social media to widen their reach, engage customers more personally, crowdsource ideas, and gather invaluable consumer data for strategizing.

2.3. Social Media as a Powerhouse for Businesses

To comprehend social media's power for businesses, let's begin with an all-encompassing figure: as per Datareportal's Digital 2021 report, there are 4.20 billion social media users worldwide, representing over half the global population. Clearly, the potential reach for businesses is colossal!

Social media has transformed how businesses market themselves and interact with customers. It's no longer about broadcasting message but about engaging audiences in meaningful conversations, fostering a sense of community.

Enter the era of social media marketing - a strategy that leverages social media platforms to promote products and services. Effective social media marketing goes beyond just posting updates on platforms. It requires in-depth understanding of the audience, extensive content strategy, and constant monitoring and analysis of the engagement metrics.

2.4. Unveiling the Potential of Social Media for Profit

Social media provides lucrative opportunities for direct monetization. Digital advertising is a prime example. Brands pay considerable sums to advertise their offerings on popular platforms, reaching millions instantly. Facebook earned about 84.2% of its 2020 revenue through advertising - a glaring testament to the enormous profit potential of social media.

Another avenue for profit lies in influencer marketing where endorsements or product placements from influencers have a powerful impact on their follower base. Subscription models, premium features, data analytics services, and e-commerce integrations are other monetization strategies employed by social media platforms.

Social media also acts as a lucrative springboard for innovative business ideas. Consider 'social commerce'; businesses leverage the power of social interactions for online shopping. Users can purchase directly on the platform, creating a seamless and interactive shopping experience.

2.5. The Future is Social

Social media has undisputedly etched its mark in our lives and businesses. But this is just the beginning! With continued technological and demographic shifts, social media's influence is bound to proliferate, unlocking uncharted territories of profit, impact, and innovation for businesses. Understanding the nuances and harnessing the power of this dynamic tool is hence a crucial prerogative for any business aspiring to thrive in this digital era.

We hope this chapter has sparked curiosity about the power of social media. Read on to discover more about the potential of a digital venture and explore and identify growth opportunities in social media. Understanding is the first step on the road to success, and with this comprehensive introduction, you are now well-prepared to delve deeper into the world of social media business.

Chapter 3. The Premise of a Profitable Digital Venture

The shifting landscape of the digital world presents a plethora of opportunities. The question is no longer whether businesses should venture into the social media realm, but how they can leverage it to drive profit. To navigate the torrent of possibilities and pave the road to a successful digital venture, it is crucial to understand the fundamental premise of running a profitable business in the realm of social media.

3.1. Grasping the Essence of Social Media

Social media is a dynamic, ever-evolving universe of human interaction where ideas compete, emotions influence, and the crowd behaves in unpredictable ways. Still, at its very core, social media is about building relationships. It is about conversation, connection, and, most importantly, an ongoing interaction with a global audience.

Building a profitable digital venture begins with understanding that social media is not just another advertising channel, but a communication platform where a narrative must be crafted with profound insight, empathy, and creativity. The profit doesn't emerge from isolated sales pushed aggressively on a prospect, but from a continuing dialogue that engages, educates, and enthralls the audience into an environment of trust that eventually leads to commercial transactions.

3.2. The Building Blocks of A Profitable Social Media Venture

There are distinct pillars that buttress the structure of a profitable social media venture. First and foremost, it is essential to comprehend that the value offering isn't just about products or services, but primarily about quality content, community, and experiences.

1. **Quality Content:** Content is the heart of a social media strategy. A catchy tagline, a visually appealing image, a thought-provoking blog post, or an engaging video can strike a chord with the audience and stimulate discussions. Properly crafted and strategically disseminated content can stir emotions, foster engagement, and inspire shares, potentially becoming viral.

2. **Community:** The essence of social media lies in its ability to build communities, a space where people can connect around a shared interest or need. Recognizing the power of these communities and participating in their dialogue can help businesses carve a niche for themselves in the social media world.

3. **Experiences:** Social media should deliver experiences and not just deliver messages. It's about telling a story that immerses and involves the audience, which is far more powerful than orthodox sales pitches.

3.3. Unpacking The Social Media Revenue Model

The revenue model in social media is multifaceted. The basic premise aligns with the fundamental traits of social media – connectivity, interactivity, and vivid storytelling. As such, revenue streams encapsulate a wide spectrum from advertising and sponsorships, the sale of goods or services, subscriptions, premium or freemium models, and data monetization.

1. **Advertising and Sponsorships:** Traditional push advertising has transformed into subtle, embedded ad content that matches the surrounding user experience while sponsorships work well when brands collaborate with popular influencers or bloggers.

2. **Sale of Goods or Services:** Here, social media becomes a direct channel for sales. Product placement posts in Instagram, Facebook Shops, and Pinterest Buyable Pins are good examples.

3. **Subscriptions, Premium or Freemium Models:** Under the freemium model, users get basic features for free while they must subscribe for advanced or special features. The success of these models bank on the delicate balance between the perceived value and the price.

4. **Data monetization:** The vast user data from social media platforms is valuable, and businesses can monetize it through insightful analytics and targeted marketing.

To thrive in the competitive landscape of social media, businesses must explore various revenue streams, assessing their viability and profitability while aligning them with their brand ethos and customer expectations.

In conclusion, a profitable digital venture on social media does not arise from spontaneous acts of sales pitches but evolves from a coherent process of building relationships, engaging customers through quality content, and driving revenue through diverse and innovative avenues. It is about creating a digital space where conversations sponsor your brand, trust sponsors your products, and customer engagement becomes your most significant return on investment. By engraining these fundamentals into the ethos of your company, your digital endeavors are far more likely to prosper in the competitive realm of social media.

Chapter 4. Identifying Growth Opportunities in Social Media

The exploration begins with a panoramic view of the thriving social media landscape. In the constantly evolving digital era, it is crucial to stay abreast of the emerging trends that have potential for profitability. We must widen our perception to include both familiar and unfamiliar facets of social media where growth opportunities may be hiding in plain sight.

4.1. The Basis: Social Media Demographics

To identify potential growth opportunities, we must first comprehend the demographics of different social media platforms. Each platform has a unique audience based on a multitude of factors like age, geography, language preference, lifestyles, education, and interests. To analyze these demographics, rely on public statistics, market research reports, or even the platform's own analytics. This is your stepping stone to identifying untapped markets, trendsetters, and prospective customers. Remember, it's crucial to understand who your audience is before you can strategize on how to engage and capture them.

4.2. Emergence of New Platforms and Features

Innovations in technology never cease, and social media is no exception. The constant introduction of new platforms like TikTok, Snapchat and features such as Instagram Reels, Facebook Live, clubhouse spaces, all open doors to novel opportunities. Embracing these enhancements early can give your business a competitive advantage. However, it's crucial to evaluate how these platforms or features align with your target demographics and overall business goals before investing substantial resources.

4.3. Recognition of Trends and Viral Content

A clear understanding and timely adoption of popular trends and viral content can propel your brand to unprecedented success. Leveraging the virality of memes, popular hashtags, and viral challenges can boost your brand awareness exponentially. However, authenticity is key. Forcing your brand into a trend where it does not naturally fit may backfire and tarnish your brand image.

4.4. Socio-Political Climate's Interplay

Engagement in current socio-political issues via 'woke' branding has been a successful strategy for many brands in recent years. By taking a stand on certain issues, a company can form a deep connection with its consumers who align with these beliefs. However, such engagement needs to be heartfelt and genuine, as consumers are quick to discern tokenism from legitimate involvement.

4.5. E-Commerce Capabilities and Monetization Paths

Most social platforms now offer e-commerce capabilities. Instagram Shopping, Facebook Marketplace, and Pinterest Shopping Ads are viable platforms for selling products. Developing a comprehensive understanding of these e-commerce facilities and other monetization paths within these platforms can provide various avenues for revenue generation. Whether it's exploring affiliate marketing, sponsored posts, or crowdfunding, you must stay informed about the monetary opportunities available.

4.6. Influencer Marketing: The Gigantic Wave

It's no secret that influencers are ruling the social media roost. Collaborations with influencers can catapult your products or services to massive audiences. Additionally, micro-influencers, typically with a follower count below 50,000, can offer significant return on investment (ROI) with their niche followership.

4.7. Data Analytics: The Guiding Light

Data analytics is your compass in the ocean of social media. It provides insights into how your content is performing, who is interacting with your posts, and the ROI of your campaigns. Analytics guide you to make informed decisions and course corrections as you navigate through your social media journey.

By understanding these factors, businesses can begin to identify potential opportunities, create a strategy, and execute it effectively. The reward? A thriving social media presence that propels your venture to unimaginable heights. The following chapters will delve deep into the strategies to leverage these opportunities and invaluable insights on developing a robust business model to ensure your social media venture is not a passing fancy, but a sustainable business.

Chapter 5. Innovative Social Media Business Ideas

While the explosion of social media platforms provides a promising landscape for businesses and entrepreneurs, the sheer number of potential business opportunities can be daunting to navigate. This chapter presents innovative social media business ideas, dissecting each with a few principles. As we traverse across this fascinating landscape, it's vital to remember that the best ideas often come from a thorough understanding of the platform and its users.

5.1. Leveraging Influencer Marketing

Influencer marketing is the modern-day word-of-mouth advertising, propped on the pillars of trust and authenticity engendered by influencers. Companies can engage influencers in their niche to endorse their offerings, expose their brand to a massive audience, and consequently influence their buying decisions.

To venture into this business idea, entrepreneurs should have an extensive knowledge of social media networks, understand influencer marketing trends, and possess excellent networking capabilities. A matchmaking platform for brands and influencers, an influencer marketing agency, or a consultancy firm offering professional advice to brands - these are just a few possibilities.

5.2. Delving Into Social Media Consultancy

With the progression of social platforms into core business tools, organizations require expert guidance in managing their social presence efficiently. A social media consultancy company provides professional help to businesses, aiming to optimize their social media strategies.

The services can range from platform-specific advice to developing comprehensive social media plans, creating engaging content, and analyzing metrics for performance enhancement. Social media consultants should have a deep understanding of various platforms, trends, and analytics, along with robust marketing knowledge and creative thinking skills.

5.3. Podcasting: The Rising Star

While podcasting may not seem a traditional social media business, it's rapidly becoming an influential platform for sharing ideas and storytelling. Entrepreneurs can take advantage of this growth by starting podcast channels on engaging topics or creating a business around podcast editing services, podcast marketing, or even a platform to connect podcasters and advertisers.

5.4. Capitalizing on Gamification

The next business idea harnesses the potent combo of social media and gamification. Applications that turn daily tasks into fun, engaging games while socially connecting users present a compelling proposition. Entrepreneurs can explore opportunities like gamified fitness apps, educational platforms interspersing social features with quizzes and challenges, or productivity tools, rewarding users for achieving goals and sharing their successes socially.

5.5. Harnessing User-Generated Content

One spectacular quality of social media is its ability to generate massive amounts of user content. Capitalizing on this, businesses can offer platforms or services that aggregate, curate, and monetize user-generated content. For example, one could build a platform that congregates travel photos and testimonials, creating an insightful travel guide.

5.6. Penetrating E-commerce Via Social Media

Social media platforms are no longer just avenues for engaging customers; they've gradually morphed into potent marketplaces. Entrepreneurs can latch onto this trend by starting a fully social media-based e-commerce enterprise – be it Instagram boutiques, Facebook Marketplace stores or Pinterest boards leading directly to purchase links. Such enterprises require strong relationships between branding, influencer partnerships, and a keen eye for aesthetic design.

5.7. Social Media Management Tools

As businesses juggle multiple social media accounts, the demand for platforms offering effective management and analytical tools is on the rise. Tech entrepreneurs can tap into this market by creating intuitive and comprehensive social media management tools that aid businesses in scheduling posts, monitoring engagement metrics, and deriving actionable insights.

5.8. Video-Based Learning Platforms

Video content, with its engaging nature and high information retention rate, makes a compelling case in the social media world. Entrepreneurs can seize this opportunity by creating platforms for video-based learning, catering to a myriad of topics - ranging from academic subjects to lifestyle skills.

Each illustrated idea, packed with potential, calls for a thorough examination and fine-tuning, considering platform-specific dynamics and audience preferences. As we transition to the next chapter on 'Strategizing for Social Media Success', it's pertinent to note that a remarkable idea, executed with an equally remarkable strategy, paves the way to social media triumph.

Chapter 6. Strategizing for Social Media Success

An effective social media strategy is a fundamental cornerstone in crafting the destiny of any business in the digital landscape. It's not just about creating innovative content and gaining followers, but more about driving targeted traffic, nurturing relationships with consumers, and turning leads into conversions. This process can be broken down into various elements: tying your goals to metrics, understanding your audience, competitor analysis, content creation and curation, building a social media schedule, and course correction via analytics.

6.1. Identifying Your Goals and Linking them to Metrics

The first stop on our journey of strategizing for social media success is identifying your goals. What do you want to achieve through your social media presence? Are you looking to increase brand awareness, generate leads, or provide customer service? Each goal can be linked to one or more key performance indicators (KPIs) which are quantifiable values that gauge the success of your strategy.

For example, if your goal is to increase brand awareness, inculcating metrics like engagement (likes, comments, shares) and reach (impression, follower count) in your strategy is key. Similarly, if your goal is to generate leads or drive sales, tracking metrics like click-through rates, conversion rates, and cost per lead will be critical.

6.2. Understanding Your Target Audience

No strategy can be successful without a deep understanding of your target audience. Knowing their demographics, psychographics, online behaviours, and preferences will help curate a strategy that resonates with them. Use the wealth of data from analytics tools offered by social media platforms to gain insights into your audience's likes, dislikes, and behaviors. Capitalize on these insights to create messaging that connects with your audience and fosters customer loyalty.

6.3. Competitor Analysis

Understanding what your competitors are doing on social media can serve as a powerful tool in honing your own strategy. Regularly monitoring their actions can not only provide you with inspiration but also preempt understanding of industry standards and trends. Try to answer questions like: Which platforms are they using? What type of content do they post? How often do they post? How do they engage with their audience?

6.4. Content Creation and Curation

Content is the backbone of your social media strategy. Valuable, entertaining, and engaging content fosters relationships with your audience, increases your reach, drives website traffic, and ultimately leads to conversions. When brainstorming content ideas, remember to balance promotional content with informative and educational ones. Including different content types – visual posts, videos, user-generated content, quizzes, polls, live streams – in your strategy is key to keeping your audience engaged.

6.5. Building a Social Media Calendar

A social media calendar is the control panel of your social media strategy, an essential tool that helps manage, curate, and schedule content. The frequency of your posts is a significant aspect of the overall algorithm of most platforms. Consistency keeps your brand at the top of your followers' feeds and minds. Your calendar should also incorporate periods for observing special events, holidays, industry-related awareness days, and any relevant dates.

6.6. Adjusting Your Strategy through Analytics

Finally, remember that the strategy that worked for you today might fail tomorrow. This is why constant evaluation and adjustments are critical. Use analytics tools to gain insights into how your content is performing, measure the success of your strategy, and identify areas of improvement. Evaluate whether your posts are reaching intended audiences, generating engagement, driving clicks to your website, and achieving all other KPIs that you defined at the start.

In conclusion, achieving social media success requires a well-thought-out and robust strategy. By identifying your goals and tying them to metrics, understanding your target audience, analyzing your competitors, creating engaging content, building a thorough social media calendar, and regularly adjusting your strategy via analytics, you can harness the power of social media to take your business to unprecedented heights.

Chapter 7. Developing a Robust Business Model

In the realm of social media business, building a robust and sustainable business model is paramount. This forms the backbone of your venture and determines its capacity to withstand volatile market dynamics, harsh competition, and fast-paced technological advancements. In this regard, proper planning, meticulous analysis, and strategic decision-making are integral factors to consider.

7.1. Constructing an Effective Social Media Business Model

If you don't have a clear, feasible, and effective business model when you enter the social media market, your business could falter before it even begins to gain momentum. The first step towards creating this model is defining what your offerings will be. These might be specific services, a unique platform, personalized content, a distinctive application, etc. Essentially, the offer should either solve an existing problem or fulfill a demand in the market.

Take the time to consider the details of your business operation. This includes projecting your operating costs, psychologically pricing your services according to perceived value, and selecting a revenue model that suits your business best. A revenue model could be subscription-based, transaction-based or centered around advertising revenue, for instance.

7.2. Identifying Your Target Audience

Creating buyer personas helps understand a target audience that would most likely be interested in the offerings of your social media business. While doing this, several factors like age group, geographic location, tastes, preferences, behaviors can be considered. For instance, a platform offering professional networking solutions may primarily focus on employed people and students in higher education settings.

You should also understand the target audience's consumer behavior as it's a useful tool in enhancing content optimization, personalizing user experience, and developing resonating marketing strategies. Tools such as Google Trends, Twitter Analytics or Facebook Analytics can be helpful in identifying your audiences and their behaviors.

7.3. Competition Analysis

Scoping out your competition is an important aspect of building a robust business model. Analyze their content, engagement, and market reputation. Can you do different or better? Also, ensure you're aware of any gaps in the market, any unmet needs of the potential customers that your competition isn't fulfilling.

Tools like SEMrush and SimilarWeb provide detailed reports on your competitor's digital strategies. Understanding their social media trends, SEO successes, and their overall web traffic strategies will help you craft a unique strategy for your venture.

7.4. Building Your Unique Value Proposition (UVP)

A UVP (Unique Value Proposition) is what differentiates your business from countless others in the market. It highlights unique strengths and innovations that set you apart. An effective UVP is clear about what it offers, directly targets the pain points of consumers, and lucidly communicates how it solves the consumer's problem better than competitors.

7.5. Deciding on Revenue Streams

At this stage of the business model development, your primary goal is to figure out how to monetize your efforts. Common revenue streams for social media businesses include advertising, sponsored content and partnerships, product or service sales, data selling, and more.

For instance, businesses can charge advertisers for ad space on their social media platforms, creating a reliable source of revenue. Alternatively, creating a network for businesses promoting related products or services can also be profitable. For example, a fitness app can collaborate with nutritionists, gyms, and workout equipment retailers, generating income by selling a space for their services.

7.6. Developing a Scalable Model

Finally, when developing your business model, consider future growth and expansion. You'd hate to build a successful venture only to find that it can't expand because the original business model doesn't allow it. Therefore, it's important to create a scalable business model. It could be expanding into new markets, offering new products or services, or scaling your operations.

In conclusion, developing a robust social media business model combines strategic foresight with careful consideration of various market fundamentals. It's not something that can be done on a whim, nor can it be successfully accomplished without adequate research, planning, and management. Faced with such an endeavor, the entrepreneur must unite a deep understanding of market dynamics, consumer behavior, competitive landscape, and innovative thinking, all while maintaining a clear vision of costs and potential revenue streams. The essential goal remains to construct a business model that not only successfully launches the venture but also sustains and assists in its growth.

Chapter 8. Omnipresent Approach: Multichannel Social Media Marketing

For a business to be successful in the digital age, it's not enough to be present on just one social media platform. An omnipresent approach ensures maximum reach and engagement with a diverse customer base, which ultimately drives growth and profitability. This approach involves the use of multichannel social media marketing – an essential tool for any business operating in today's interconnected world. We delve into this rich topic with comprehensive detail in this chapter, presenting you with an in-depth understanding and a guide to successful multichannel marketing strategies.

8.1. Grasping the Concept of Multichannel Social Media Marketing

Multichannel social media marketing refers to the strategy of engaging with your audience on multiple social media platforms. This can include Facebook, Instagram, Twitter, LinkedIn, YouTube, Pinterest, TikTok, and more. The idea is to expand your reach by tailoring your message and approach to fit the unique characteristics and audience of each platform. Businesses use multichannel marketing to connect with consumers across different stages of their buying journey and foster stronger relationships.

8.2. The Importance of Multichannel Social Media Marketing

The rise of the digital age means that the traditional approach of focusing on a single marketing channel is rapidly becoming obsolete. Today, the average consumer uses several platforms, and adopting a multichannel approach presents multiple opportunities to engage these consumers.

A multichannel approach helps a business:

- Improve its visibility and reach across diverse platforms.

- Effortlessly track consumer behavior across platforms, gaining valuable insights.

- Strengthen customer relationships by offering multiple touchpoints.

- Enhance brand consistency by delivering a unified message across different channels.

8.3. Constructing a Multichannel Social Media Marketing Strategy

Building a successful multichanel strategy can be divided into four primary steps:

Step 1: Understand Your Audience Start by understanding your target customers. Do thorough research to determine which social media platforms they use and when they are most active. You should also understand their content preferences, and whether they engage more with videos, images, text posts, or other types of content.

Step 2: Create Unique and Tailored Content Each social media platform boasts a unique user demographic and usage culture.

Therefore, your content should reflect this diversity to maximize traction and engagement on each platform. For instance, short videos are more suitable for TikTok, while in-depth articles are more fitting for LinkedIn.

Step 3: Integrate All Platforms To wield the full power of multichannel marketing, integrate all your channels, ensuring your brand voice and messaging stay consistent. You could use social media management tools to schedule posts and monitor performance across platforms.

Step 4: Test and Optimize Evaluation and optimization are crucial steps in any marketing strategy. You can use analytical tools provided by most platforms to measure post engagement, feedback, and other metrics. Use this data to guide future strategy, tweaking any elements that aren't working and building on those that are.

8.4. Embracing Technological Tools for Effective Multichannel Social Media Marketing

Emerging technology has made it easier for businesses to manage, measure, and optimize their multichannel marketing efforts. For instance, platforms like Hootsuite, Buffer, and Zoho Social can help businesses manage multiple social media accounts simultaneously, analyze performance, and schedule posts in advance. Meanwhile, other tools like Google Analytics and Facebook Pixel help track user behaviors, providing valuable insights that can shape your overall marketing strategy.

8.5. Challenges and Solutions in Multichannel Social Media Marketing

While multichannel marketing offers tremendous benefits, it also presents unique challenges. These can include maintaining brand consistency across platforms, dealing with divergent platform algorithms, and managing the increased workload resulting from handling multiple channels.

Automating certain processes using social media management tools, adopting a systemic approach to content creation to ensure consistency, and leveraging data analytics to understand and adapt to the algorithms can combat these challenges.

In conclusion, an omnipresent approach in multichannel social media marketing is an invaluable strategy to capitalize on today's vast digital landscape. It extends brand reach, engages customers at various touchpoints, and drives growth. Remember to familiarize yourself with your target audience, tailor your content to individual platforms, integrate your marketing efforts, and regularly evaluate and optimize your strategy for maximum impact. Armed with this knowledge and a suite of digital tools at your disposal, you're ready to conquer the dynamic world of social media marketing.

Chapter 9. Scaling Techniques for Your Social Media Business

As the world becomes increasingly connected, it's vital for businesses to leverage social media's potential to scale and reach larger audiences. The journey from starting a social media venture to scaling it successfully can be complex and fraught with challenges; however, with the right strategies and an understanding of how these platforms work, the journey can also be fulfilling and profitable.

9.1. Focusing on Your Target Audience

First and foremost, to scale a social media business, it's critical to understand who your target audience is. Invest time and resources in comprehensive market research to understand your audience's demographics, preferences, needs, and behaviors. Utilize social media analytics to fine-tune your approach and tailor your content accordingly. An understanding of your audience will allow you to create more focused and engaging content, ultimately driving higher engagement rates and growth.

9.2. Creating High-Quality, Engaging Content

Quality content is the cornerstone of any successful social media venture. Craft content that is not only engaging but also provides value to your audience. This could involve educational content, instructive how-tos, inspiring stories, or interactive quizzes and polls.

Furthermore, remember that visual content is particularly effective on social media. High-quality images, videos, infographics, and live streams can significantly boost your engagement and reach.

9.3. Establishing a Strong Social Media Branding

Make your brand recognizable and consistent across all the platforms you use. This includes maintaining a consistent tone of voice, visual aesthetic, value proposition, and brand message. The more cohesive and identifiable your brand identity, the greater trust and loyalty you will inspire in your consumers, leading to long-term growth.

9.4. Engaging with Your Audience

Encourage and maintain an open dialog with your audience. Respond promptly and thoughtfully to comments and messages, regularly ask for feedback, and be willing to engage in conversations on your platform. This will position your brand as approachable and consumer-oriented, further fostering trust and loyalty among your audience members.

9.5. Utilizing the Power of Influencer Marketing

Influencer marketing can be an effective strategy for scaling a social media business. Work with influencers who align with your brand's values and appeal to your target audience. Influencer endorsements can provide a significant boost in visibility and credibility, accelerating your growth.

9.6. Leverage Algorithm Changes

Every social media platform uses algorithms to determine what content to show to users. Therefore, understanding these algorithms is critical. Regularly update your strategy based on algorithm changes and mold your content to maximize visibility and engagement.

Discussed open-endedly, these sub-topics offer intricate insights into the science and art of scaling a social media business. Between balancing content quality and understanding your audience, creating an identifiable brand, and leveraging algorithm changes, it is clear that there are various components to the formula of success. However, by integrating these strategies into a comprehensive plan, any business can unlock the potential for exponential growth on various social media platforms.

Standing at the intersection of technology and communication, social media delivers unique opportunities to scale businesses and reach global audiences. The key to leveraging its enormous potential, however, lies in understanding its intricate mechanisms, recognizing its changing landscape, and adapting your strategies accordingly. The results, undoubtedly, make the journey worthwhile – a journey of continued learning, consistent effort, and adaptability, propelling your venture towards unprecedented heights on the backbone of social media. Take the leap, immerse your venture in these techniques, and prepare to explore uncharted territories of massive success and unparalleled growth.

Chapter 10. Sustaining Growth Amidst Social Media Algorithm Changes

Contemporary digital marketing is a lot like trying to sail on shifting waters; the course frequently shifts, demanding continuous navigation and strategic modifications. As we step into the realm of sustaining growth amidst these constant shifts, particularly those triggered by social media algorithm changes, it presents a thrilling yet challenging expedition.

10.1. Understanding the Impact of Algorithm Changes

Social media platforms are perpetually modifying and optimizing their algorithms. Facebook, for instance, steers clear of saturating user feeds with promotional content, opting instead to offer content that fosters meaningful interactions. Instagram's algorithm particularly values user engagement, while Twitter prioritizes relevancy and timeliness of posts. Algorithm changes are driven by an ambition to enhance the user experience. However, they can impact the visibility, and thereby, the success of a business on social media. Grasping these changes and adapting to them swiftly can be key to sustaining and enhancing your company's growth.

10.2. Adapting to the Changing Algorithms

How then, do you adapt to the turbulent seas of social media algorithms?

10.2.1. Developing Adaptive Content

The first step lies in developing adaptive content. Businesses should strive to create engaging, high-quality content that resonates with their audience and encourages interaction, thereby making the most of the social media algorithms that prioritize high engagement. As algorithms evolve to prioritize content that promotes meaningful interactions, businesses should ensure to generate content that nurtures conversation and interaction amongst users.

10.2.2. Customer-Centric Approach

Focus on employing a customer-centric approach. Since algorithms are formulated to enhance user experience, center your content around the consumers' wants and needs. Regularly surveying your audience to understand their changing preferences can help in crafting content that resonates with them, further amplifying your visibility on these platforms.

10.2.3. Diversifying Social Media Portfolio

Diversify your social media portfolio so as to not be overly reliant on one platform, minimizing potential disruption when algorithmic changes occur on any single platform.

10.3. Navigating through Algorithm Updates

Navigating through constant updates can seem daunting, but certain strategies can help your business stay ahead of the curve.

10.3.1. Staying Informed

Stay well-informed about the algorithm changes on various

platforms. Regular monitoring of updates from the platforms themselves or seeking information from credible industry sources can ensure your business isn't caught off guard when changes are implemented.

10.3.2. Experimentation and A/B Testing

Experimentation allows you to understand the practical implications of the changes implemented. Conduct A/B tests to determine the optimal content strategy in response to the recent algorithm changes, as such changes can largely impact the success of different types of content.

10.3.3. Measuring Performance

Keeping a close eye on metrics and KPIs is integral. Monitor your engagement rates, reach, conversions, and other key analytics consistently to evaluate the success of your strategies and make the necessary course corrections.

10.4. Ensuring Sustainable Growth Amidst Change

Despite the challenges, algorithm changes can present valuable opportunities for businesses to innovate, optimize, and grow.

10.4.1. Building a Strong Community

Building a strong community of engaged followers ensures that your content remains visible on their feeds, irrespective of the algorithm changes. Regular interactions with the community, responding to comments, and encouraging dialogue can foster this relationship.

10.4.2. Leveraging User-Generated Content

User-generated content can boost your visibility and reach. Encourage customers to share their experience with your brand which not only builds virality but also increases the perceived authenticity of your brand.

10.4.3. Paid Advertising

While organic growth is critical, paid ads can also complement your marketing strategy. Since paid content is not affected by algorithm changes, it can be a reliable way of ensuring visibility.

Sustaining growth amidst social media algorithm changes is a continuous journey. It demands agility, a deep understanding of the changing tides, and astute navigation skills. The turbulent waters might be difficult to navigate, but with these strategies, your boat is well-equipped to sail smoothly and seize the opportunities these changes bring along!

Chapter 11. The Future of Social Media Business

In any journey, voyaging the terrain of the future requires a vigorous understanding of one's present and a compass to navigate the uncertainty. In the case of social media business, this compass takes form in the blend of thorough trend analysis, cautious prediction, and agility to adapt.

11.1. A Look Into the Crystal Ball: Upcoming Trends in Social Media

Today, social media is more than a place for people to connect; it has become a thriving marketplace and an essential tool for businesses. With the evolution of these platforms into sophisticated marketing, sales, and community-building utilities, business owners must stay atop of emerging trends. As per the current trajectory, we foresee five possible trends for social media business.

1. Rise of Ephemeral Content: First introduced by Snapchat, then adopted by Instagram and Facebook, ephemeral content (posts that disappear after a certain period) has proven immensely popular. This trend feeds into the desire for authentic, in-the-moment engagement that captivates audiences. The future seemingly favors more such content, pushing businesses to master short-lived storytelling.

2. Surge in AI Integration: Artificial Intelligence (AI) is transforming social media marketing by providing insights from a massive pool of data and shaping personalized consumer experiences. With improvements in natural language processing and machine learning, AI is set to offer even more precise recommendations and predictions effectively driving business decisions.

3. Virtual Reality (VR) and Augmented Reality (AR): As 5G becomes mainstream, social media platforms can harness the power of increased bandwidth to deliver immersive VR and AR experiences. This trend could spawn a new wave of interactive advertising opportunities for businesses, creating more engagement and closer connections with customers.

4. Prominence of Social Commerce: Social media will continue to bridge the gap between discovery and purchase, making social commerce a behemoth in the business world. The incorporation of new features such as Instagram's 'checkout option' hints at a future where social media could potentially replicate, if not replace, traditional e-commerce platforms.

5. The Shift Towards Private, Interest-Based Communities: As users seek more personalized and interactive experiences, the establishment of private, interest-based communities will flourish. These are spaces for businesses to cultivate loyal customer bases, drive deeper engagement, and gain insights about their target audience's needs and preferences.

11.2. Adapting to the Social Media Business Landscape: The New Gameplan

In this evolving digital landscape, businesses should adopt proactive, multifaceted strategies for survival and growth. To aid in this challenge, here are a few seminal strategies:

1. Content Diversification: As tastes and preferences change, businesses that can swiftly adapt their content will thrive. A diversified content strategy includes long and short videos, interactive posts, stories, and user-generated content, among others to maintain the audience's interest.

2. Investing in AI and Analytical Tools: The ability to extract

actionable insights from data is a game-changer in a competitive social media landscape. Investments in AI and other analytical tools can help in targeted marketing, personalized recommendation, and smarter business decisions.

3. Building Customer Communities: Fostering a sense of belonging through private, interest-based communities enables businesses to drive up customer loyalty. By leveraging such spaces, businesses can evolve with their customer preferences and needs.

4. Seamless Shopping Experiences: The future will favor businesses that can align their social media strategies to facilitate a seamless shopping experience. In essence, reducing customer journey touchpoints by integrating discovery and checkout processes is vital.

5. Stay Informed and Flexible: The fast-paced world of social media requires businesses to remain agile. This entails keeping up to date with the latest trends, being open to experimentation, and having the ability to pivot strategies when needed.

11.3. Future-proofing Your Social Media Business Against Algorithm Changes

With constant updates to social media algorithms, businesses must adopt several key practices to maintain organic reach and engagement. Here are a few useful tactics:

1. Emphasize Engagement: Platforms prioritize content that sparks engagement. Thus, creating compelling posts that encourage likes, comments, shares, and saves is essential.

2. Dive into Data: Regular analysis of your engagement metrics, demographics, and other relevant data can inform the

development of a more robust social media strategy.

3. Cultivate Relationships: Actively engaging with followers, responding to comments, giving shout-outs, and sharing user-generated content can strengthen relationships with your community.

4. Prioritize Video Content: Video content generally gains better organic reach than text and images. Experimenting with various formats such as live videos, IGTV, or Reels can extend your reach.

5. Optimize for SEO: Many social media platforms now function similarly to search engines. Optimizing your profiles and posts for search can increase your visibility.

Although the roadmap to the future is paved with uncertainties, businesses equipped with the right strategies and foresight can weather shifts and seize opportunities in the evolving landscape of social media businesses. As we forge ahead, the world of social media continues to promise an exciting commercial playground, blending creativity, connectivity and commerce into a potent mix for success.